Words That I Can't Say
A Workbook For Journal Therapy

Oh Huishan

All rights reserved. No parts of this book may be reproduced or transmitted in any form or by any means, electronic or mechanical, including photocopying, recording or by any information storage and retrieval system without prior written permission from the author.

Copyright © 2010 by Oh Huishan

Cover design by Oh Huishan
Front cover royalty-free artwork by Fotolia.com

Title: Words That I Can't Say —- A Workbook For Journal Therapy

Author: Oh Huishan
Editor: Oh Huishan
Publisher: Lulu.com

Printed in the United States of America

ISBN: 978-0-557-61040-2

Author email: huishan@insing.com

For all those people out there who long for and hope to see rays of sunlight emerging through the dark clouds. You will get there!

HOW TO USE THIS BOOK

SECTION I

Part 1 and Part 2 are two chapters meant to be the longer chapters filled with my personal experiences in life along with ideas and topics for you to write in your journal.

SECTION II

Part 3 to Part 17 are shorter chapters that are meant for you to touch and go.

This book is about my story which I use to make examples of things to think about in your life. It is part memoir part journal therapy workbook.

I hope you will find something in this book that speaks to your heart!

Contents

SECTION I
Part 1: An Introduction — 1
Part 2: Role models — 13

SECTION II
Part 3: Remembering your childhood — 22
Part 4: Fiction therapy — 25
Part 5: Making a difference — 28
Part 6: The time of my life! — 30
Part 7: Work! Work! Work! — 33
Part 8: Mistakes and regrets — 36
Part 9: The leap of faith — 39
Part 10: Secret letters — 42
Part 11: Coping with deterioration — 44
Part 12: Body image — 47
Part 13: Craft & Hobbies — 49
Part 14: Relationships — 52
Part 15: The strength to go on — 54
Part 16: I have the dreaded illness! — 56
Part 17: Forgiveness — 59

ABOUT THE AUTHOR — i

Acknowledgements

I would like to thank the Goddess of Mercy, otherwise known as Guan Shi Yin Pu Sa to Chinese people, for being the spiritual anchor in my life. Without Her I would still feel very lost spiritually. Having Her as my Protector and Guardian makes me feel very blessed indeed.

I thank my mom especially, who was my only caregiver and held my hand whilst I walked through darkness and emerged into the light, always by my side.

I also thank all family members who had been there for me in life when I needed them, including any acquaintances and friends.

I would like to give my special thanks to 2 doctors when I was struck with psychosis. Dr. Theresa Lee, who had been the best psychiatrist I ever met and whom had given me the best care possible while I was hospitalised in IMH. Dr. Marcus Tan Wee Lun had also been the very best with me during my 2nd hospitalisation at IMH.

The nurses and doctors I have met in my life had mostly been very good to me. I thank them all for their patience and care!

SECTION I

Part 1: An Introduction

This is a personal journey I'd like to share with my readers. Journal therapy for me started as an outlet, a means for venting my innermost emotions, thoughts and feelings when I was going through some extremely tough times. As I have learned, even when you give anonymity to family members or friends by not writing their names on the Internet, people still get offended when you write about them in your personal online blogs. There is of course the freedom of speech everyone has but it has put me off of writing about my true feelings towards other people on online blogs except maybe reviews on music or celebrities. I will still touch on the topic of blogging in this workbook as it is undeniably a social phenomenon that is becoming an everyday life necessity for people all around the world.

I long to express myself truly, and I don't want the fear of people attacking me on blogs about my views. Therefore I have gone back to the good ole personal journal in physical: a pretty notebook and trusty pens. Sometimes I feel like nobody would ever know about my feelings I have inside of me. Counselling provides a platform for me to express myself and it is definitely kept confidential. I get the feeling of having someone know about the matters of my life and I will therefore not die in vain when

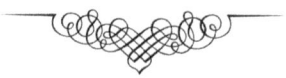

my time is up. I have so much to say and no one to listen. Counsellors give me a sense of security. Well, only the counsellors who work well with me and understand me give me a sense of security.

It's the things that I don't say out loud that bothers me, I guess. I like plugging in the earphones and listening to music while I journal. It shuts out other noises and I sometimes don't like the awful silence, although you may actually like quietness to calm yourself. There are times I find it hard to express myself in my journal. I get so "constipated" with all that is happening I can't even begin to imagine how I could possibly let it all out in the most orderly fashion possible.

Even if I do tell what is bothering me to my mom just to let it out, I don't usually know how to handle the emotions that come with it. What I do at this point, which happens to me quite a lot during trying times, is to jot down short one or two liners in my journal about the matter and the feeling I have about it at that point of time.

After a while, when I am calm and collected, I look back at the small notes in the journal and I think about what the underlying issue was that bothered me enough to produce such a strong reaction.

Blind optimism becomes debilitating while perpetual depression is unhealthy. Thus I will ask questions that will make you reflect upon both the

good and the bad so if you feel this is not what you believe in then by all means choose the things that do resonate with you.

In journal therapy, one important factor is that if you are working with a therapist, the therapist is supposed to help guide you to find your own answers. There must be total honesty in your personal journaling because you will have to reflect upon what you have expressed and analyse the situation from "outside the situation you are in" in order to realise certain truths that you were blind to when you walked around in circles. The expression of self comes first in journal therapy.

Reflections happen when you are mentally and emotionally ready to face your past or when memories are triggered. Memories can sometimes bring forward those repressed feelings and emotions you have and cause some uncomfortable reactions. You can be your own therapist but if there are issues that you feel personally unable to handle, it is always a good idea to have a professional therapist or counsellor around to hold your hand through the process. Look up your local professional counsellors in directories or online popular search engines such as Google or Yahoo. If all else fails, contact your local crisis hotlines. You are not alone.

The materials or things needed for you to start journaling

Physical journaling will mean that you need to find a paper notebook or diary and pretty pens if you like. Choose those that fall within your financial budget. It is preferable that you find something which you can easily bring around with you. I like to decorate my paper journal with some stickers or pretty things. You can find a lot of decoration tips from the Internet and books. Martha Stewart is a good example of creativity as well. You will definitely find refreshing tips from her on her website.

Electronic journaling might also include mobile phones and PDAs (personal digital assistant) other than the traditional blogging websites or software.

You have to decide for yourself if your personal journal is "for your eyes only". Take care of your privacy and level of comfort in disclosure of your journal details to anyone else. It applies to both physical and electronic forms of personal journals.

Blogging on the Internet

Blogging can be such a joy but responsibilities must be explored when using this mode of expressing your thoughts, feelings and emotions. Electronic

Frontier Foundation has written a "Bloggers' Legal Guide" on their website and it consists of guidelines to help bloggers know their parameters and rights. EFF is the leading civil liberties group defending your rights in the digital world (www.eff.org). This is one of the most comprehensive and user friendly resources for knowledge on blogging ethics I have come across.

The convenience of blogging helps create a "room of your own" online with personal preferences in the design and colours of your blog at a click of your mouse. Blogs are very organized and you can find your posts in the archives easily. In this IT era, many people are turning to blogging instead of paper and pen to journal their thoughts. Some people still feel more personal with paper and pen but if you are concerned with environmental issues, you might support blogging because it saves paper.

For me personally, I prefer my paper notebook because I like to look at my own handwriting and I feel a bond between me and my personal journal that way. I've tried blogging but as I have mentioned, I find it a bit restrictive because I can rant and rave about anything or anyone at all in my paper notebook, which I never show anyone else, and not get in trouble with someone or even the law. Of course, you can choose to lock your blog up and make it a private blog and that is totally up to you. You call the shots.

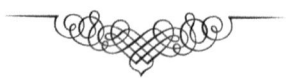

So... What do I write?

When you have chosen your mode of personal journal, you can start writing entries straightaway. The easiest way to start off is a list of things that are on your mind which affects you at that point in time. You can do a "good stuff" and "bad stuff" inventory in point form. After that, choose the ones that you really feel strongly about and elaborate on them.

I absolutely love doing inventories. That is one of the most important tips I can give you. When everything is in a mess and your thoughts are conflicting with your feelings, doing an inventory can give you an overall picture of what is actually going on. When in doubt, always start off with an inventory. You can even elaborate in the form of mind maps after you have written down your lists. Organization helps you to rationalize things and situations.

> *People around you are usually not professional counsellors. You wonder why they never listen...*

I seem to have a knack for making people run the other direction by telling them too much information than they can take or process. I forgot

the fact that they are not trained professionals in counselling. Most people have enough problems in their own lives and you could actually overload them by your attempt to let it out of your system, that is if you have very big problems. Of course if there are receptive friends or family members, you should indeed share your feelings with them.

When things really started getting to me after a long period of time struggling to make sense of things, I decided to get help. I went for professional counselling and undergoing therapy was fantastic, even if there were only a handful of sessions as I dropped out when too much things boiled up to the surface that I was not ready to face.

Nonetheless, things started falling into place. Hurt feelings were soothed as issues were handled with rational thinking and feedback from the counsellors helped me to see things with new eyes.

Your personal journal is your own best friend. No matter what, it is always there for you. You do not need to fear that it will criticize you or judge you. The whole world can misunderstand you but never your diary.

Journal therapy does not replace a listening ear per se but it is very, very helpful. It goes hand in hand with different ways of therapy for the self.

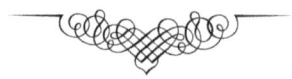

Famous journal writers

Anne Frank is probably one of the most famous journal writers ever. I have never read her book before but I got my hands on a BBC adaptation TV serial "The Diary of Anne Frank" starring Ellie Kendrick as Anne Frank. I wanted to know what Anne Frank was all about and I have to say, I cried a lot watching it. I could feel Anne's need to feel free in her writing amidst all that chaos happening around her. I guess it really spoke to me because I felt almost the same way when I was journaling to feel a sense of security amidst the illnesses happening to me. Of course I also understand my psychosis and journaling does not compare to Anne Frank's dire straits in the World War II while she did her journaling.

Anne Frank is an absolute inspiration. She is a legend. What happened to Anne Frank was that she was in hiding together with her family and some other Jews as Adolf Hitler was hunting down Jewish people to persecute them in the World War II in Europe. Unfortunately, Anne Frank's hiding place was betrayed and the Nazi police, the Gestapo, rounded them up and after the Nazis' surrender ending the World War II, only Anne Frank's father, Otto Frank, survived the war. The people who helped Otto Frank to hide his family and friends managed to keep Anne's diaries and loose leaf notes which she wrote during the hiding

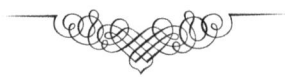

and returned them to Otto. He managed to later on publish Anne's work and the rest is history.

Samuel Pepys was an English naval administrator and Member of Parliament, who is now most famous for his diary. His influence and reforms at the Admiralty were important in the early professionalization of the Royal Navy. The detailed private diary he kept during 1660-1669 was first published in the nineteenth century (*Wikipedia*).

Music to my heart

Have you ever been inspired by music? The feelings that arise from listening to songs that I love inspire me to write. Choose music that suits the mood or purpose you have and listen to it while you write in your journal. I love Maxwell's "Whenever Wherever Whatever". The melody is soothing and it lulls like a lullaby. Treat your life like a movie and you obviously need a "soundtrack" for your movie.

Count your blessings

When I am feeling really sad and depressed, it can be rather overwhelming and it "blinds" me to what I have right now. Counting your blessings may be a good exercise to do. Write down the good stuff that you have in life and in possession right now in point form. Make sure these are things that are important

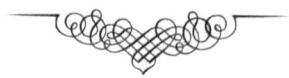

to you. Just put the negative situations and bad things you have right now to one side, you don't need to write those down for this example.

Example A:

1. I have a new laptop.
2. I have a new television.
3. I have access to the Internet.

And the list goes on… You can then elaborate on how these good stuff make you feel and maybe their purpose.

Example B:

1. The new laptop gives me so much joy because I can write my books with it and I can look at pretty pictures saved in the laptop. I can also listen to my favourite mp3s with it. It is a personal space I cherish. I don't know how I can live without my laptop.
2. The new LCD television replaces the old one that was spoilt. I can watch Entertainment Tonight at 6pm on Channel 5 every weekday and it makes me excited to know all about the entertainment news they have daily. I can also watch that very nicely written Taiwanese television drama on weekends together with mom and dad. My family and I need our daily dose of Chinese news broadcast in the evening

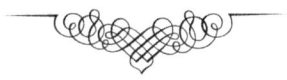

as well. Sometimes newspapers are just not enough!
3. The Internet connection I have is a major blessing. I don't feel lonely when I'm on the Internet as I know I can reach out to the world on it. I don't have a room of my own at home as we have a small apartment but having my laptop and broadband makes me feel I have a space of my own to call home.

These are some examples to show you how to go about making an inventory and a more detailed elaboration to understand what does and does not make you tick. Of course you do not need to have perfect English to be able to express yourself effectively in your journal. I don't write in full sentences in my journal half the time. Publishing a book requires a certain standard of English and unless you want to publish your personal journal details as an autobiography or memoir, there is no need to feel ashamed of your capabilities in expressing yourself.

In the following chapters of this workbook, I will include more food for thought and exercises which will provide you with topics to write in your own journal. Life is beautiful. And so are you.

Exercise 1:

Have you thought about what you want in life right

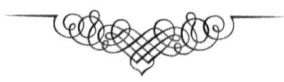

now? How about setting some short and long term goals about your desires? Is negativity taking over your daily life? Do you need to analyse your own thoughts? Do the good and bad inventories. Get to know yourself better by revealing your innermost feelings in your personal journal. It is a start.

Part 2: Role models

I think that when you are lost in life and don't know what direction your life might lead to, it is very useful to have role models to look up to. It does not matter whether you are in a good or bad part of your life, as long as you are a ship out there in the dark, a lighthouse is what you need when you want to anchor near land safely.

I found an incredible book and I treasure it a lot. It gives me hope and warms my heart whenever I read any of the stories on the individuals who became famous and yet have gone through life's difficulties and continued to persevere to become the best that they could be. The title of the book is "The secret of success is not a secret: stories of famous people who persevered" and the author is Darcy Andries.

Darcy Andries started out wanting to inspire and motivate her special education students by sharing stories of famous people who had succeeded in life despite of failure in any form. She ended up having a few hundred stories and later decided she would compile all of these stories into a book. Eventually a publisher agreed to publish her book.

Some of you might feel overwhelmed by this book as it has a collection of stories of more than 300 people. I am approaching this book step by step, reading a

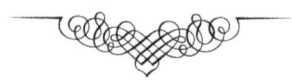

few stories a day. This is a book you can go back to whenever you feel the need to be inspired. I felt touched over and over again but I had to take a lot of breaks reading it because I was so emotional but in a good way. If you feel like nobody ever took notice of you because of all the failures that had happened in your life, this collection of inspirational stories will bring you hope and renewed faith in yourself.

One person who inspires me and gives me conviction to live my life to the fullest is Viktor Frankl, who was coincidentally mentioned as well in Darcy Andries' book. His pregnant wife, brother, mother and father all perished in the concentration camps they were in. Viktor Frankl had survived 4 concentration camps in World War II when he was a young man and lived to be 92 years old before passing away in 1997 due to heart failure. Viktor Frankl was an Austrian neurologist and psychiatrist. He was also the founder of logotherapy, a form of Existential Analysis, which was sometimes called the "Third Viennese School of Psychotherapy" after Sigmund Freud's psychoanalysis and Alfred Adler's individual psychology. I will explain further the reason behind why logotherapy and Viktor Frankl inspire me in *Part 5: Making a difference*.

Obviously, when people used to tell me, " Huishan, think of all the people worse off than you are! You won't feel so depressed anymore. It's your approach and attitude towards things around you that you need to change!", I would feel even more depressed.

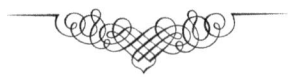

That was just the way I was. I felt more depressed thinking about people who were more disadvantaged than me because I felt deep sympathy for those people. I'm very emotional about things. For those of you who do believe in horoscopes and zodiacs, I'm Scorpio. It does seem to fit me, the way Scorpios are talked about. Intensity of thoughts and emotions are traits of a Scorpio. I don't just look at myself as a Scorpio though, what is most important is that I realized I must become more of myself. I am a bigger picture than what a Scorpio is. It is a bit safer to just moderately believe in horoscopes because ultimately, it is you who is in control of your behaviour and life in general. I had courage that I never knew was inside me. Opening up to other people after the string of unfortunate events in my life seemed sometimes easy and at other times difficult.

Ellen DeGeneres is another role model I look up to. She is so hilarious! It really perks me up when I visit her website and watch those latest videos of her show online. Humour is a lifeline for me. I know it is kind of cliché but laughter is the best medicine! I'd be feeling depressed and inconsolable about my feelings of uselessness due to my illnesses and when I go watch her video online, I laugh like a hyena! Well... sometimes! I guess most of the time I just snigger and chuckle.

I needed to have role models so badly back in those days when I was embroiled in my own chaos but I was not anywhere near being able to conceptualize

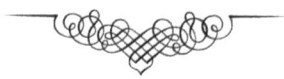

anything or be cohesive in my thinking. I kept fighting the voices in my head. At first, I kept my earphones plugged in the whole day, everyday, listening to the radio and trying to drown out the voices that disturbed my clarity. Then at times, the voices would threaten to harm me if I don't do what they told me to do. I felt so lost. I felt as if the voices were me and I was nothing. Something deep inside me shone through and said, " I have to become more of myself. Even if the world was coming down on me, pick up a pen and a notebook and just write! Write anything at all!"

I was writing a lot of rubbish but when there were moments of clarity in my writings, it was like a mirror reflecting who I truly was to myself. I don't understand myself but I looked at them with awe.

" Did I write that? Where did that come from?" I immediately remembered the reaction. It was the same when I was in secondary school. I always wrote things I did not think was possibly from myself. I knew then that I had a talent in writing back in those days. I just never recovered from the shock of only getting a grade C5 for my English in the "O" Levels as I was among the top writers in the class I was in. And no, I was not practising "channelling of light beings" during my secondary school days. So the things I wrote were truly from deep within myself.

It took me so many years to become sober in my mind as I am now ever since it all started in 2004. I

felt so trapped for all that time because the voices were the ones whom were in control of me. I did not like that and I personally did not condone it. At first, psychosis was a scary diagnosis. It sounded like I was some "psycho" on the loose. Hallucinations, hearing voices, paranoia about someone or something trying to harm me all the time were just some of the things that happened when you have psychosis.

I remember I had asked one of the psychiatrists before if I was mad. The psychiatrist said no. " Being mad is when none of the medication or therapies actually works and the patient is immersed in the state of not knowing what was truly reality or imagined."

I started to look for jobs when I could hold a conversation fairly well without stammering or having fear on my face all the time. Nobody would hire me when I said I had mental illness. The rare few who did not mind allowed me to hold a job but it was usually too physically strenuous for me. The fact that I had low morale did not help me to hold down the jobs long enough. Sometimes I would work for only 2-3 days which meant that I was unable to receive any pay for that short period of time working. I would sometimes also quit and not turn up the next day by just calling up the manager or supervisor. I spooked easily and I felt really fragmented. The only time I lasted in a job for a month after I had psychosis was as an office cleaner in Shenton Way.

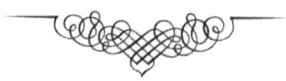

There had been psychiatrists, nurses, work placement agents who had suggested that I keep my mental condition confidential when looking for jobs. I still have to go for follow up every 3 months to get my medication. What was I supposed to say to my employer about all those hospital appointments? I did not like withholding the truth but I also understood about what they meant as there is still stigma in the society about mental illnesses. Even writing about my experiences in this book is kind of frightening because I do not know how readers will react to it. Maybe I'll just be words on pages for my readers and not reveal any photographs of myself. That might work.

My memory was really very bad after I was diagnosed with psychosis. I had forgotten how to use Microsoft Excel almost entirely, considering I was good enough to use it to plot scientific graphs while I was in a local polytechnic before I dropped out. I tried over the years to relearn Excel but after 3 courses, I still did not remember how to use Excel once the classes were over. I had even achieved full marks for the test in one of the courses I had taken up with NTUC Learning Hub. That was only when I was in the class. Not long after I just did not know what to do with Excel yet again.

It was because of this that I could not succeed in finding a job as an administrative assistant in an office. Being a cleaner sometimes took what was left

inside me physically and I would not be able to go on with the job. I decided I would become an author because writing was the only thing I could still do and remember amidst my bouts of amnesia, which was somewhat like Dory's problem in "Finding Nemo".

It was so bad, I sometimes did not know whether I had showered or not and had to constantly ask my mom whether I had done it. Mom was my only caregiver. At one point she had to quit her job to look after me full time. There were also very depressive moments which constantly led me to become suicidal. Although I hated being hospitalized but I was glad that eventually after 2 hospitalizations and some adjustments to the doses of medication I was taking, I finally settled on a proper dosage which made me normal as long as I kept on taking it correctly.

Now that I am more sober, I realized how scary it can be to become moodily suicidal. I had felt that no one in the world cared and that I was so alone. The chemical imbalances in my brain were wrecking havoc and physical situations in reality sometimes did not help. Personally, I would recommend anyone who feels remotely suicidal to speak with a professional counsellor or call up your local crisis hotline. I gained a lot of caring from people who worked as nurses in the hospital and they showed me that even if you felt you were unloved or that nobody cared, they still cared about you. If I needed help

with my adult diapers, the nurses were sometimes impatient but they did their best to help. I had urinated in the hospital bed because I was so scared of the voices I could not walk to the toilet to do it. I was around 23 years old when that was happening.

When I read the stories from Darcy Andries' book lately, I would sometimes cry quietly, feeling those tears again on my cheeks. I felt numb for the last 1-2 years as I was all cried out. It felt good that I could actually cry again.

I feel really useless a lot of times because I wished I could help my parents financially instead of them supporting me because I cannot find work. So I decided to dedicate most of my free time to writing. At least I am doing something useful and not wasting away my time in life. I am a workaholic like that.

The simple act of writing down Viktor Frankl's name in my personal journal serves as a trigger for me to feel more determined about not letting things bog me down emotionally. You don't have to write a full essay in your personal journal to have an effect of inspiring motivation. It can also be very useful if you write down what feelings you have when you see the name of your role model in your personal journal. You will be reminded of your convictions whenever you reread your journal entry.

Exercise 2:

Write down a list of role models you admire in your personal journal. Elaborate briefly what is it about these people that inspire you. If you like, do mind maps about it. What do you want out of life for yourself? What are some of your desires and dreams? How will the motivation you get from thinking about these role models bring you to where you want to be?

SECTION II

Part 3: Remembering your childhood

Reminiscing your childhood memories can give rise to positive or negative feelings. For some, it can bring a smile to your face, feeling fully nostalgic. For others, it can be rather traumatising or unpleasant. Personally, I do enjoy thinking about my childhood.

Mom could not afford childcare for me so she brought me wherever she worked. There were times when I helped wipe the wet forks and spoons mom washed while she worked as a maid in some terrace houses nearby our HDB apartment. I did not know how I managed to keep still and be quiet while mom worked but I did. Some of the bosses were kind enough to let mom bring me to their houses and she had assured them that I was very obedient and would not cause any trouble while I waited for her to finish work. Mom said I would sit quietly in the living room and wait patiently.

It was the same when mom changed jobs. When mom worked as a food stall assistant in a foodcourt, I would sit on the chair that was directly in front of the stall mom was working in and stayed there till she knocked off. I never spoke to any strangers and I made sure mom could always see where I was. There was also a time when mom worked as an ironing lady

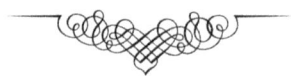

in a flatted factory and I sat listening to the pocket radio just outside the door of the workplace and I could smell fresh bread being baked in flatted factories just opposite the building. I dangled my legs from the chair and sang softly to the songs I was listening to. Mom also dropped me off at my grandma's place for my relatives to watch over me while she worked although I cannot remember how old I was when I was at grandma's.

Those were happier times for me. Although I did not have a table at home to do my homework on, mom brought me to KFC and I would finish my schoolwork almost daily there. I had straight As for my primary school leaving exams, the PSLE, except a C for mathematics. I guess when I went to secondary school, I could not cope with the pressures of puberty. I felt easier as a child.

I could take a lot of stress as a kid. I admired that about myself when I think of those days. It seems almost like another lifetime to me. How did my childhood shape me into who I am today? It is not like I never had luxuries in life. When I was a teenager I had some luxuries because my eldest sister was working at that time. I wished my positive traits from childhood had survived my period of puberty but I think they were lost amidst the desires of gaining peer support, which ironically did not turn out very well either.

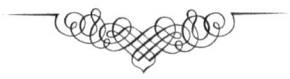

My doctors had told me that my hormonal imbalance and chemical imbalances in my brain was probably due to an improper development during puberty. I was very depressed as a teen and I never really thought much about it. Maybe if I nailed it earlier on in life, it would not have gone into such a full swing when I was a young adult.

Exercise 3:

Did your childhood bring you happiness or sadness? What were the pivotal moments? How has your childhood influenced you as you grew older? What do you wish to change about yourself right now that remains from childhood? What traits did you have from childhood you wished you still had? Think about the people who meant the most to you when you were a child. Are they still around? Do you wish you had cherished them more than you had?

Part 4: Fiction therapy

Sometimes writing down the actual events which had caused trauma or unpleasant memories may be a daunting task. You can actually write little short stories in your personal journal, creating fictional characters who had similar life experiences. You could also let them play out scenarios whereby you wished you had done if you had a second chance. It will lead to a sense of closure for issues or situations you felt were beyond your control.

Writing short fiction to express your deep felt unhappiness and sadness gives a sense of anonymity and that allows you more room to work with your issues.

Example:

Georgia's husband walked out on her and their 2 kids after she was retrenched due to the bad economy. She felt betrayed and overwhelmed with anger and sadness. She was so depressed she felt there was no hope for her. Her kids were all that she had. Her savings were going to run out soon. Just then her best friend, Sandy, suggested that Georgia should go for counselling and offered to take care of her kids for a while, while Georgia straightened out herself.

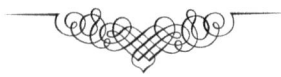

Georgia felt the raw pain in her heart whenever she thought of her husband and what he did. While attending counselling sessions every week, she started journaling her feelings by writing short stories with fictional characters who were going through what she was going through. It was just too much to even see her husband's name on paper. It cut her deep. So fictional characters with new names felt more "detached".

"Mandy's husband left her. She was so in pain when one day she ran into her husband again in the supermarket. She took up a cooking utensil and went straight for his body. She slapped him and then beat him up with the utensil in her hand. He suffered cuts on his face and backed away, running out of the supermarket. Mandy dropped her weapon on the floor and sat down crying."

Georgia felt the euphoria of being able to get back at her husband through her fictional short stories.

This example shows you how you can use your imagination to build a healthy mental and emotional state by using fictional writing as self therapy.

You can do a myriad of things with fiction therapy. The sky is the limit!... No, the galaxy! You know what I mean.

Exercise 4:

Write a list of issues and situations you feel strongly about that sort of haunt you on a regular basis. Create fictional worlds and characters who are ready to take your place and do your bidding. No one has to see what you write. Feel free to unleash your sense of justice and right the wrongs that have been done onto you. Write about regrets that are finally resolved. Embrace yourself and reward yourself for your courage to face these issues.

Part 5: Making a difference

Finding meaning in your life is important but sometimes even the healthiest and happiest people find this search a mystery. And while you are still searching, you can do a lot that adds meaning to life in general, whether it is for your life or the lives of other people. A kind word, a kind act and maybe even volunteering your services for the needy ones can let people feel the love and kindness you have for them. Unwittingly, by your simple gestures, someone else finds meaning in their lives. Isn't that amazing?

Logotherapy, which is founded by Viktor Frankl, focuses on the need for a meaning in life for humans. Logotherapy is not a new age concept. It is a type of psychotherapy.

[The notion of *Logotherapy* was created with the Greek word *"logos"* ("meaning"). Frankl's concept is based on the premise that the primary motivational force of an individual is to find a meaning in life. The following list of tenets represents the basic principles of logotherapy:

- Life has meaning under all circumstances, even the most miserable ones.
- Our main motivation for living is our will to find meaning in life.

- We have freedom to find meaning in what we do, and what we experience, or at least in the stand we take when faced with a situation of unchangeable suffering.]
(*Excerpt from Wikipedia*)

Knowing that we can make a difference in other people's lives can be very empowering. I encourage you to get a copy of Viktor Frankl's bestselling book " Man's Search For Meaning" which chronicles his experiences of the Holocaust and how it became a basis for the creation of logotherapy as a type of psychotherapy. This book changed my life. Prepare for tissues while reading this haunting book!

Exercise 5:

Think about the miserable times in your life. Can you think of anything that came out of it that had meaning? Do you think that if you are successful as a person right now, that the bad times might have shown you what not to do and created a foundation for you? Has it taught you how to turn your failures into success? This journal entry might be very encouraging for you to reread again and again when things are not going well for you. It will tell you that there is meaning even in the worst times of your life.

Part 6: The time of my life!

What brings a smile to your face? What is it that makes your heart sing? Happy times in our lives can mean so much to us. Having an optimistic outlook in life is great too! As long as it is not blind optimism, a healthy sized ego can be essential in perseverance of our desired goals in life. Sometimes, it is not necessarily thinking about good things that keeps you positive and inspired. Thinking about the bad things that could happen or have happened and making sure you don't make the same mistake twice can be a very good level of reality check too!

I used to think that as long as negative thoughts were out of my system, I would be attracting only positive things into my life. I overlooked reality checks on myself and relied very heavily on the idea of being able to pursue a path of enlightenment spiritually through new age concepts and beliefs. Maybe a lot of people who were in the new age movement knew how to keep grounded amidst all that curiosity in the supernatural but I obviously was going off the track with all that was happening.

For a while I thought that was the happiest time of my life until everything spiralled out of control. I can safely say that now that I have put all that behind me, the happiest time of my life is right now!

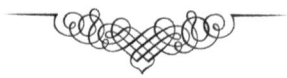

Through the hard times, I realized how important my mom was to me and how much she had sacrificed just to help me to get back on track and become well again. When I was really depressed because I could not find a job, I asked mom why she did all she could and made me more sober. Maybe if I was still "loopy", it would justify the fact that I cannot be hired. Mom said I could at least take care of myself if I was sober. She also said that I could become sober again because I worked on it meticulously, otherwise without the will to get well, I could never have become sober again.

Right now I am grateful I am very sober compared to the times when I was hospitalized. I can be a full time author! Being able to dedicate the whole day to just musing over my life and listening to the radio, then switching on my laptop to write my book is probably the best thing that has happened to me so far.

Every other door for me was closed except the one that makes me an author. I sleep when I want to sleep and wake up when I want to wake up. Life is so good to me! The truth is, if I don't sleep well, I naturally feel depressed again. I just have to figure out the timing for the daily 3 meals… My breakfast is usually 1pm. I know, I sleep lots: lots of drowsy medicine.

Exercise 6:

What are the most memorable happy times in your life? Do you wish there were more of these in your life right now? Does happiness mean the same to you right now when compared to the past? How has it changed? What is that one thing you can do now that will make you happy?

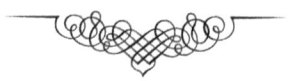

Part 7: Work! Work! Work!

Are you a workaholic? Or do you procrastinate about everything? It does not matter whether you work as a checkout girl or boy, or even a high flying executive. As long as you put all your heart and effort into your work, you will have tried your best. Sometimes work can be very stressful and if you are unemployed, the worries you have may even weigh very heavily on you and give you emotional and mental distress.

For those who have work, remember to chill out after work. Maybe you can make a list of things that will cheer you up despite the work stress. Having a cup of your favourite Ice Blended from Coffee Bean or hitting that nearby bar with colleagues and friends might just perk you up! Time management may be a part of your working problem if you always feel you do not have enough time to do all the things you need to do. You can prioritise your work under 3 categories: low, medium or high urgency. In this way, you will know what is more important and needs to be attended to immediately, rather than looking at all the tasks piled up on your table and have sleepless nights over it.

For those who are unemployed, maybe you need to reassess your situation and list down your talents and skills you have through the years of work you have accumulated. Maybe you would also like to see if it is financially possible to go back to school and retrain yourself in another new skill to stay competitive in the current workforce. Keep on trying to get work when you have the strength to persevere. Send out all those revised resumes and know that someday soon, the job meant for you will come.

And for those who have the right ideas, the support and the finances, maybe self employment might work for you! You could note down all those great ideas and mini plans in drafts in your journal. These points may expand to a business proposal.

I started out trying to write a collection of short stories previously and I had never ever written a book at that time. It was so hard to squeeze out so many ideas and write for so long! I guess that really worked as a warm up for me to write this workbook. It does not feel daunting anymore to write books and I feel that the flow goes easier every time I write something more. I try my best to Google the internet and go to the local libraries to research or find inspiration to write new material right now, right here. I am making my writing my own job, sort of a "self employed" job I guess.

Every moment is an inspiration, and I hope I never run out of that.

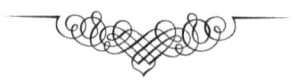

Exercise 7:

Can you think of what makes you happy about your current job? Maybe these reasons might help you become happier with your job! Is unemployment a state of fear for you? Maybe you are going through a rough patch with finances and personal relationships due to unemployment. Have you approached your local departments or organizations that help people to redevelop skills or do job matching? Are your business ideas feasible? Have you gone on to research on the market demand for whatever your idea is? You can share your happiness or sadness with your journal and it will be your private confidante!

Part 8: Mistakes and regrets

There are probably some things which you wished you never did. I had my own share of mistakes and regrets and if I had a chance to do it all over again, I would have done it differently. It is okay to feel broken, you just need to seek help when you are ready.

If only I had noticed that my depression during my teenage years had gone on too long or if I had not gone into new age practises due to my love for X Files, I probably might be a regular adult having my own job without mental illness pulling me back. I was feeling depressed, sick with hormonal imbalance and wanted to feel like I belonged and so I went for meditation classes. Being able to see unicorns and angels in my meditations got me hooked on the desire to meditate often. I pursued a lot of new age things because that feeling of magic was in the air and it made me euphoric emotionally which was a stark contrast compared to my depression.

I was running after the unicorns in my mind and I did not realise that I was beginning to handle things improperly being unrealistic in my beliefs. I know those of you out there who are fine and have been practising new age concepts and have never

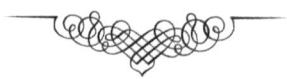

encountered the "off the track" side of new age things are probably thinking I am giving new age practises a bad name. You are free to follow whatever practises you feel most comfortable with. All I am saying is that whatever happened was my personal mistake. I should have gone to consult a psychiatrist for my depression instead of getting hooked on seeing unicorns in my meditative state because chemical imbalance was causing my depression instead of just simple life issues.

It is really important for parents to watch over what their young children are doing in terms of spirituality. Lord of the Rings, Harry Potter and many fantasy or science fiction shows are great to watch for entertainment but when it causes a rash decision to try out witchcraft for real without the supervision of trained professionals, it can be very dangerous. You never know what you are dealing with. In the western world, witchcraft might be very common and if you are an adult and you do make a decision to follow it, at least research about it properly before you commit to anything. This applies to any spiritual practise or religion you plan to go into.

Everyone has their own regrets and any time is a good time to address them, especially if it is controlling your life. The mistakes of the past do not have to go on for the rest of your life, if you can help it. On the other hand, if it is a wiser action to not resolve your mistake or regret due to probable

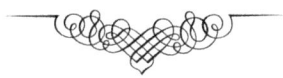

negative outcome, you do not need to act on it but you can definitely write about it in your journal.

Exercise 8:

What are the mistakes you have made that still haunts you? Do you have any regrets weighing on your heart? Write down what you want to do about these if you had a second chance. Even writing about it helps to release your emotions. Keep in mind that you will need to learn how to grieve over things and memories of the past and then when you are done, let these regrets rest in peace and move on with life.

Part 9: The leap of faith

Right now, all that matters to me is the leap of faith I am making. Being a full time author means that I would not be able to have basic finances while writing the book and it will only come in after the book sells. It is all a matter of whether this book is an okay read and also whether there is divine intervention with divine blessings for the future course of this book and my career as an author.

Have you ever taken a leap of faith in your life? Sometimes because of that, we crash and burn and at other times things do get better. And when the results are disastrous, you go through shock to find out that it does not work out and then you panic. Fear crawls into your heart and you go into denial. Anger overwhelms you slowly and you go through a phase of beating yourself up for having done the leap of faith. "How could I be so stupid? I can't believe myself!" Or maybe denial is stronger and you think to yourself, "Why me? Why does it always have to be me?"

So what if nobody believes in you? Maybe you needed those mistakes to lead you onto the path that had the special door opened and which had been awaiting your arrival into a new phase of your life! I guess it is really true when people say, "Things happen for a reason." Even if you made the wrong

leap of faith, believe in yourself. Pick yourself up. Tell yourself it is okay to fumble sometimes. Learn to be kind to yourself.

Funny how I kept seeing Viktor Frankl mentioned in the books I borrowed from the local library to research on ideas for this book. The number of coincidences have caused me to think that it is more like what new age people might say, "It is synchronicity! Not coincidences!" Maybe… Maybe not. I would like to think that they are little road signs for me to tell me I am on the right path by Goddess of Mercy, whom I pray to. And that is why I am thinking maybe this book might be good enough, even for a first attempt.

I truly hope that people take a chance on me and believe in me. I do believe in myself amidst all my doubts but it really would help if just one person believed in me other than my own journal. I was writing about my doubts on a forum online and a kind stranger told me that she was proud of me and my effort to move forward even though I had so many odds against me and she said she is waiting to read my book when it is finished. I was so touched! I did not know that by all that I was doing, I was moving forward. I thought I was running around amok. It is okay to doubt I guess, just don't drown in it.

Exercise 9:

If you have someone you can confide in, maybe you should run by that person about what you believe might be a good leap of faith in your current situation. Maybe you could try to imagine together with that person, what kind of good and bad scenarios might come out of it? Is it worth the risk? Hopefully it will not a blind leap of faith. And if you do not have someone to talk to at all and the matter is of utter importance, you might want to approach a professional counsellor. After all that, write about your new experience in your journal and include past occurrences regarding any situations that required a leap of faith. Analyze the situations a little.

Part 10: Secret letters

Do you have something to say to someone but the circumstances just seem to disallow that? Fret not. You can actually write secret letters addressed to that particular someone without ever sending it or letting that person know!

There could be a myriad of emotions going through you as you create those secret letters and it would be wise to allow yourself some breaks in between if you are overwhelmed. I have personally written some secret letters which I had later on thrown away as an act of letting go.

Burning secret letters might not be a good idea, well at least not for me. Most Chinese people burn incense papers to deities and ancestors and so burning letters might mean that roving spirits might get them instead, which is why I do not dare to burn those letters. But if your culture is okay with that, by all means burn the letters and give the intention of letting go of the issues you have with that person and then let nature take its course.

You can write secret letters to people who bully you, people whom you dislike or hate, people who matter to you the most and maybe people who don't understand you. You could also write secret letters to your pets! Unleash your creativity.

I write secret letters to Goddess of Mercy. You could write to Jesus or the Buddha, depending on what your spiritual or religious beliefs are. You could also write to your deceased loved ones if you feel like you miss them or if you did not have the chance to tell them something important when they were still alive.

Secret letters are the secret thoughts and emotions that were buried deep within your heart. Find a chance to let go of them in the gentlest ways possible, if circumstances allow. Being bottled up could seriously harm your health whether it be mind, body or spirit.

And maybe someday when you look back at some of the secret letters that you still keep, you might have moved on emotionally into a healthier place within yourself.

Exercise 10:

Use different coloured pens or pencils to write your secret letters. You could choose different colours to represent your different emotions.

Part 11: Coping with deterioration

I remember the times when I was younger between the age of 16 and 19 years old. I had worked as a temporary cashier in 2 departmental stores. I experienced Christmas long queues and another major sale period. My memory was very good and I was well versed in swiping credit cards and settling cash payments. I had also worked in a major boutique of a well known brand, which was very popular, as a part time boutique assistant. I never slacked and was very hardworking.

Then came some illnesses, including mental illness later on. One manager at a small shop said in a roundabout way that I was slow and too blur when I tried to work after mental illness struck. When I said I was going to quit immediately, she changed her attitude and said that I could learn things slowly and everyone did not start out knowing a lot. I quit anyway. I discovered that especially because of my mental illness, my memory was very bad and my response time was indeed slow, even if it does not seem that way from my external appearance. Cleaning jobs were giving me rashes all over my body because I have sensitive skin and eczema from birth. Sometimes certain cleaning jobs required a lot of work, depending on each company's work

delegation. I decided to stop looking for cleaning jobs. I was freaking out after a few days at work as my fingers were too itchy and painful.

I used to be such a good worker and now I am just probably a liability. I kind of understand how it feels for old people. Deterioration can really make you feel trapped inside your own body, watching yourself change from being competent to being a dependant.

Have you had experiences where you were not as good as before anymore? Deterioration can be in so many forms. The common thoughts that might go through your mind could be "I am so useless! I'm a good for nothing!". Of course, negative thinking does not help the situation but it is a good indication about what you are feeling deep inside if you work backwards from your thoughts to your underlying issues.

It really helps if you can try to think creatively on how to handle your situation. For me, I decided to write something everyday instead of just lying on bed all day long doing nothing. Can you think of something to do that makes you feel that you are using your time productively? It does not have to be something bombastic.

The bottom line is, if things are not rosy anymore for you, learn to be kind to yourself.

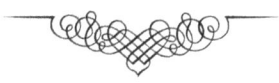

Exercise 11:

Do you have anything about you that is deteriorating, compared to your past? Does it hurt your feelings? Are you a "youngster" or are you a senior citizen? How can you help yourself to feel better about your deterioration? Think about ways to go about your situation without deterioration affecting your life.

Part 12: Body image

Are you satisfied with the way you look? How is your body image like? I used to be slim at 18 years old but after I was being treated for polycystic ovary syndrome and hormonal imbalance, I ballooned a lot. Through the years due to mood swings, comfort food and medication induced weight gain, I have somewhat developed an inferiority complex about the way I look. It really does not help that with my eczema, every time I try exercising, I will have breakouts of rashes all over my body due to intensive sweating. I do try to take walks though but I guess I must really change the way I eat to have any weight loss going on.

I have had times when I hated the way I looked but after learning to be kind to myself more due to dealing with my mental illness, patience towards myself has become very important in my life. You don't need to be slim to have things happening in your life. It can start right away, right now! Who says you can't look good if you are plus size? I have seen so many plus size women on the streets nowadays who look like plus size models. They are so hip and happening!

If you are sad about your body image whether it is because you are too fat, too thin, too ugly, too anything at all, stop right there now. You can make

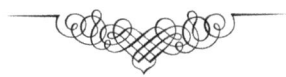

your life happen right now! Who says you need to be perfect just to go to that café? Or maybe you thought, " If only I was slim and turned heads, maybe I might get that perfect job or perfect partner!" And while you wait for yourself to become what you visualize your perfect self to be, how have you wasted time between then and now?

Right now, what is important to me is that even if I am wearing an old t-shirt and bermudas, I am happy the way I am. Because if I despise myself, I will never be able to start living!

Exercise 12:

Collect pictures of yourself through the years. Which are your favourite ones? If you have the finances, you could hire an image stylist and shop for a new wardrobe. Or hitting the online blogshops that sell clothes and accessories of your size could prove to be effective shopping therapy. But first, give yourself some respect and a pat on the back for being willing to take the first step towards appreciating the way you look now.

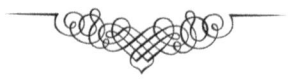

Part 13: Craft & Hobbies

I do apologise if I have been sounding out of the weather, after all, writing this workbook is a cathartic experience for me too. Something miraculous happened and it has lifted up my mood and I guess it is like a daily rainbow for me. I saw that there are people teaching teddy bear making and bag and purse making! I am so excited! Although I had 2 experiences in making small soft toys when I was a teen, I had never truly embraced the full on field of craft and hobbies. I barely passed art classes back in secondary school. I never was good at sketching or painting but I am rather pleased with the way I designed the front cover for this book so I guess my artistic talents lie in different kinds of expressions.

I love the way James Taylor sings "It's only a paper moon"! This song really expresses the mood I am in about teddy bear making, especially the part where the song goes, " But it wouldn't be make believe if you believed in me". I am awaiting the birth of my line of teddy bears from my hands with eagerness, helping them to come alive! Well, that is if I finally do get around to taking up the classes but it is definitely on my "to-do" list.

I was almost apprehensive in the past when the topic of crafting came up. I felt like an idiot in home economics classes back in school although there were a few things that piqued my interest. I am no Martha Stewart but I would like to begin to learn to be one, a small one. The most amazing thing is, I have been wanting to learn how to make a purse and bag for a few years already and I have never really been able to find lessons that were right for what I wanted. I saw a teddy bear making class write up on the main website for local community centres but there were no more vacancies. I started looking for bear making classes in Singapore the past few days and I actually found a teacher who conducts classes privately in her residence for bear making and purse/bag making too! Her lessons are very affordable too! I truly believe this must be divine intervention!

I want to turn into a beautiful crafting butterfly instead of being fearful and sad in that hard chrysalis!

Exercise 13:

Taking up hobbies can help you to cultivate healthy past times. Write about your own achievements and advancements of your favorite hobbies. You might even set up a business on the side dealing with your hobbies. For example, some people make building car models a lucrative business from a simple childhood hobby. Maybe you should enter contests that are related to your hobbies too! Crafting is more

popular overseas than in Singapore but I guess this trend is slowly picking up in different ways nowadays. Of course there had been the friendship band times, the cross stitch days and the handmade jewelry blog shops of today which indicate the different tastes of people in different times. Go pick up some craft magazines and start doing something that catches your attention! You never know, it might become your next income stream.

Part 14: Relationships

We all have relationships whether they be work, school, friends, family or the significant other. Sometimes it is hard to balance it all and it is a good topic to journal about.

Normality is like a fairy tale for me, it feels so out of reach. In this case, I have no friends to talk to and sometimes there are things that my parents won't understand even if I confide in them. My current character is very hard to connect to because I am like an overstretched rubber band. I feel autistic sometimes. Despite that, building good relationships with your family is important but it depends on a case-to-case basis. Sometimes people just don't get along and you don't have to right everything that happens between the individuals.

The total opposite should happen to almost everyone else, meaning you should have a few friends you can talk to and whom you especially treasure in your heart. Show the important people in your life how much you appreciate them. It helps your loved ones to know that you value them.

Office politics can be so hard to handle and when I was in a job at 18 years old, I tried my best to stay out of it. I only concentrated on doing my job well at the boutique. I know sometimes it might be against

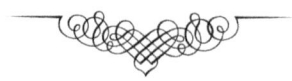

your wishes and you were somehow embroiled into tricky situations. Try making statements or decisions for the greater good of everyone.

And if you felt that you should upgrade your people skills in order to improve your work performance or to handle relationships better in your life, you could always try out reading books on emotional intelligence or attend EQ workshops or classes. I am still trying to understand the dynamics of EQ topics.

As for relationships in school, if you have a good sense of humor, it does add popularity in your life. I had more friends during pre-university days but as time went by and we all became adults, I guess people do drift apart, especially for those who got married and had kids! I miss the school days when everyone of us laughed from one end of the campus to the other. Those were the days!

Exercise 14:

It is so easy to dish out positive advice to other people but the dynamism of relationships can be so complicated sometimes. What relationships are you satisfied with in your life right now? It can be work, school or personal relationships. How do you think you can improve on them? Are there relationships you feel you should end? Hopefully you can let someone down gently if you have to end your friendship or any other type of relationship.

Part 15: The strength to go on

Do you feel like giving up right now? Are you crying yourself to sleep every night? The strength to go on is so important. It can do wonders. Every time you feel like it just isn't worth it anymore, look within yourself. Do you see that sparkle of hope anywhere at all? I guess it may all seem so cliché but you can make a resolution to break out of any situation that does not do you well. It is a matter of gathering yourself up from all those feelings and emotions and without thinking too much, begin to lift yourself up from the bottom most despair.

You can do it. Well if you feel you can't, pray. Divine intervention is possible, no matter what your religion is. Maybe your kids make a good focal point for you to trudge on through the mud. Maybe that dream you have had after all this time is so near now, being within your reach. Don't give up.

I know. It is so easy to say something positive but is it going to work when you practice it? Some times the right thing to do needs so much repetition until you notice it. Dusting yourself off after a fall and getting back up on your feet requires courage. I guess we all need encouragement when things get harder or our

path is laid with many obstacles but with that single smile from someone dear to you, it might just do it!

When bad things happen to people, they sometimes come one after another. Being caught off guard means unpredictable behaviour and reactions towards the situations. You have to hang on to something to remain afloat. Be it an unfulfilled dream that helps you to keep the faith or the smile and hug of your child or your lover, think it through and find something that perks you up and stay with that thought or image in your mind. Just breathe…

Exercise 15:

What are things that you will regret missing if you decided you do not want to go on with the things in your life anymore and become totally despondent? What are the things that drives you forward?

Part 16: I have the dreaded illness!

So what happens when you do get the dreaded illness: mental illness? The mental illness stigma is so great that even sufferers are scared of themselves from time to time. We freak ourselves out! Then at other times, I wonder why people look like they have seen a ghost when I do reveal to them that I have mental illness. It is indeed a total irony.

Almost everyone fears of getting mental illness and that fear strikes you deep inside and gets even worse when you do get it. What do you do after you are diagnosed with it? I was in denial when it first happened. I guess that was only natural. I did not want to take any medication when I was first diagnosed. The 2nd year was disastrous due to a more severe relapse because I was not on medication. This time I relented and started on the medication routine which has lasted till now, and I will keep doing it to keep my mental illness under control. I will have to be on these types of medication on a long term basis. I don't know about anyone else but for myself, the medication keeps me "normal". Well I can function as a normal person with around 90% accuracy. The 10% is for minor relapses and amnesia as well as bad memory.

There have been quite a number of people who had suggested that I try natural ways to help reduce my dosages etc. What if I get bigger relapses? I don't want to suffer from all that confusion and go through all that mental, emotional and physical pain all over again. Yes. I am scared of giving natural therapies a chance because if I get another major relapse, I would have to be hospitalised again. I don't want that to happen. I'll just drink more water to get the huge doses of medication down my throat, thank you!

It also takes a lot of courage to fight the mental illness and its control over you. People tell me to be positive about it and they usually relate positivity to being happy most of the time. That is a bit hard to achieve, I think, even for normal healthy people. I guess for me, it is a weird mix of pessimism and positivity behind the driving force of the decision to help myself get well. Most of the time, I am depressed and pessimistic with this illness but that actually pushes me forward because that is why I want to feel well and be happy, even if it is for a little while only. Then while still being depressed, my mind says, "You can do it. Just one baby step at a time."

I thought to myself, "Are you sure all it takes is one baby step at a time?" I was doubtful but it was totally logical. I was in a total mess and wrecked. There was no other way but to walk out of the labyrinth I was trapped in, one baby step at a time. I concentrated on learning to cross the road again with mom

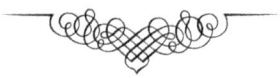

holding my hand. I did not know how to cross the road because I felt like I was in a warp in another dimension and the cars on the road were just a jpeg image. My mind was in a chaos and I was out of touch with reality.

I also had to learn how to go up and down the stairs of bridges again after the 2nd hospitalisation. The steps looked like 2D and I kept feeling like I was going to roll down the stairs if I missed a single step at all. Also, during the hospitalisations I had, I was incapable of bathing myself, just like a lot of other mental patients in the same female ward. We would line up and wait for the health attendant auntie to shower us. I was more stable after a few days and then went into the shower cubicles myself.

Now, when I look back upon myself, I wonder what ever happened to me. It all feels like a dream… Like it was a very, very bad dream.

Exercise 16:

What illnesses have you ever had that freaked you out? What were the seriousness of those illnesses? What were the reactions of your family and friends towards your illnesses? Are you wondering how you can recover from it? Note your feelings about these and give attention especially to how you can change your experience by finding the meaning in it. (*Refer to Part 5 for a reference to finding meaning in life*)

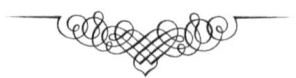

Part 17: Forgiveness

Have you ever done anything that you beat yourself up for? We all need to learn to be more forgiving, especially towards ourselves. You live 24/7 with yourself and if you harbor grudges about yourself, how do you go on living your life in peace? And that also contributes to negative commentary playbacks in your mind about the situations related to the issues that bothered you.

I have had my own share of mistakes in the past and there was a time in my life that I kept blaming myself for everything that happened. My counsellor looked at me during therapy and said, "You were very young then. You need to acknowledge that and grieve over the hurting past then move on forward when you are ready." I nodded in silence and thought about that comment. I was indeed young then. Right now, since I have gone through so much, my way of thinking has changed.

Making peace with myself was hard but I managed to do it. At the end of the day, forgiving is alright as long as you don't forget because you would not want to repeat the same mistake twice. The kind of forgiveness that is done in blind optimism can be slightly dangerous and so you need to have some reality checks first before going ahead with it. Also, it is a personal choice. You can forgive or you can

choose to hate yourself for the rest of your life. But is it worth it?

Exercise 17:

Write down a list of mistakes you wished you never made. What are the feelings and issues that are involved in these mistakes? Do you need therapy to work things out with professional help? Making the first step to starting therapy for yourself with professional counsellors or psychologists can be a major turning point for your life. You can always back out if you are not ready to face it, or you could ask for the speed of therapy to slow down to a comfortable pace. If you are feeling rather depressed, please talk to someone whom you can trust. If not your family and friends, then maybe the SOS hotline in your area or country.

ABOUT THE AUTHOR

Oh Huishan was born on 31st October 1981 in Singapore. She attended the schools Teck Ghee Primary School, Deyi Secondary School, Jurong Institute and Singapore Polytechnic. She dropped out of Jurong Institute and also Singapore Polytechnic due to health problems and bad grades. Between 2001 and 2002, she was diagnosed with hormonal imbalance which caused menorrhagia. It affected her health leading to bad grades, which was also due to affected concentration during classes.

Later on in 2004, she was diagnosed with the severe chronic mental illness, psychosis, due to chemical imbalances in her brain and she was hospitalized both in 2004 and 2005. She lost a lot of her basic functional abilities and skills and she constantly heard voices and saw hallucinations. Huishan was also hospitalized later on in various public hospitals throughout the years for different health problems.

She experienced a lot of obstacles in her life path which led to deeper depression and nobody in her social circle really understood what she was going through. Her mom was the only person who took the time and effort to cater to her needs to become her only caregiver, even when Huishan was so far gone in her early stages of psychosis because only Huishan's mom understood her.

Huishan was involved in a lot of self harm when her psychosis relapses were very severe. She would bang her head on the walls many times or hit her head with her fists. There were other times when she would roll in bed for a long time in agony and utter pain, talking to herself and the voices she heard that were not there.

During this time, Huishan survived a suicide attempt when the voices encouraged her to do so as she was in utter despair. Nobody knew if Huishan could be well again as becoming healthy again looked like a goal too far away to achieve but that little voice within Huishan amidst all the other voices said to her that she could do it and she resolved to try her best, even if she could not remember who she was or what she was doing as her memory was so bad due to psychosis.

Huishan's weight problem also worsened throughout the years. Firstly, her weight had always been in a yo-yo stage from childhood but that was okay. When she first took some medication for her menorrhagia, she ballooned an extra 10kg within one week due to the hormonal medicine. Everything went downhill from there on. Whenever she was discharged from her hospitalizations through the years, she craved outside food so much that she often binged and had frequent meals until she was very overweight.

She took up Christianity to try out if it would give her some sense of peace and calmness amidst her chaotic life and it did help in the beginning but

she felt that there was always something missing and it was no fault of the religion of Christianity. Huishan then decided to devote herself to Guan Yin or Goddess of Mercy instead and it has helped her life to become better. To her heart, maybe her affinity with Guan Yin was greater and so that was why everything seemed to fit perfectly.

A handful of people had been encouraging Huishan to write a book and she tried out writing fiction in some pretty A5 sized notebooks. It helped to exercise her mind and memory, plus she gained more confidence in her writing again. It was the only thing that came naturally for her. This book, "Words That I Can't Say" will be her first self published book.

When she first had psychosis, she could hardly speak normally and she could hardly write in proper sentences. Huishan had prayed to Jesus everyday and Jesus did help her get better somewhat. Then when she switched to Guan Yin, she prayed to Guan Yin everyday and her path felt much smoother and obstacles seemed to be lifted out of the way and that allowed her to move forward with ease. She will have to be on long term medication for psychosis as there is currently no cure for this mental illness but it helps her to function like a normal person.

Gaining certification to become a certified stress management coach with Spencer Institute is a joyous thing that has happened to Huishan. She wanted to try out the distance learning

enrichment course to train up her memory and coherence in her mind and she received a grade of 98 out of 100 for the major test. Although she wanted to learn more about managing stress for herself and others, she prefers to write books to help other people with their lives as she is still not very comfortable to face a class full of people and teach them in person.

It became very, very difficult to find a job for Huishan after psychosis hit. When she was stable enough somewhat to look for a job, she got so much rejections her mom suggested to her to become her own boss. Huishan had tried out cleaner jobs on and off but it was too physically challenging for her due to her bad physical health. Whilst Huishan dreams of becoming even better in her memory right now to take up a dressmaking course to sell her own clothes online, the idea of self publishing this book kept coming up. She decided that maybe it was a reminder from Guan Yin that she should finish and edit this book and present it to the world. It would indeed be a very big personal achievement to become an author before she hits 30 years old in 2011.

Huishan is excited about this book and she hopes that through the distribution channels Lulu.com provides in the GlobalReach distribution service, many more will get to know about this book. Being available on Amazon.com would be a dream come true for her and she looks forward to the release of this book in the later part of 2010.

Huishan lives in Singapore with her parents and her mom continues to be her only caregiver.

If you would like to contact the author, Oh Huishan, you can do so via her email at huishan@insing.com